PIANO ALL THE WAY...

NEW EDITION
Revised and Expanded

Level One-A

by

WILLIAM GILLOCK

WILLIS MUSIC

EXCLUSIVELY DISTRIBUTED BY

HAL•LEONARD® CORPORATION

7777 W. BLUEMOUND RD. P.O. BOX 13819 MILWAUKEE, WI 53213

PIANO ALL THE WAY

(Level One-A)

Foreword

PIANO ALL THE WAY is a multi-key course of study written and composed for the beginning piano pupil. It is designed to present the fundamental concepts of theory and a wide style-variety in literature, leading to musical understanding and independent reading. In addition to the basic text, the reinforcing series THEORY ALL THE WAY and TECHNIC ALL THE WAY (which correlate, unit by unit, through Levels One and Two) are recommended, as well as supplementary solo pieces; for the ultimate goal of studying music through any instrument is to achieve *total musicianship* and a reasonably adequate *performance skill.*

Level One-A of PIANO ALL THE WAY is a *pre-note recognition* series of musical experiences. In addition to presenting the concept of pulse, geography of the keyboard and ear training, the following *reading* experiences are learned:

      1. Directional reading.

      2. Rhythmic patterns involving ♩, 𝅗𝅥, 𝅗𝅥·, 𝅝.

      3. Tempo and interpretative indications.

      4. The slur and legato playing.

      5. Finger numbers.

When actual note recognition is introduced in *Level One-B* and pursued in *Levels Two, Three* and *Four,* the student is able to give his full attention to this new problem without the complexities of rhythmic beat, interval recognition and basic physical coordination — thereby reducing the hazards of discouragement and failure.

The author wishes to acknowledge with gratitude the many helpful suggestions of Louise Wadley Bianchi, Director of the Piano Preparatory Department of Southern Methodist University, Dallas, Texas, and Mildred R. Dalton of Topeka, Kansas.

William Gillock

W.M.Co. 11162

Unit 1
THE KEYBOARD
NOTES
RIGHT HAND, LEFT HAND

When you start piano lessons there are three pictures
to study before you play your first piece.

Picture No. 1 --- THE PIANO KEYBOARD

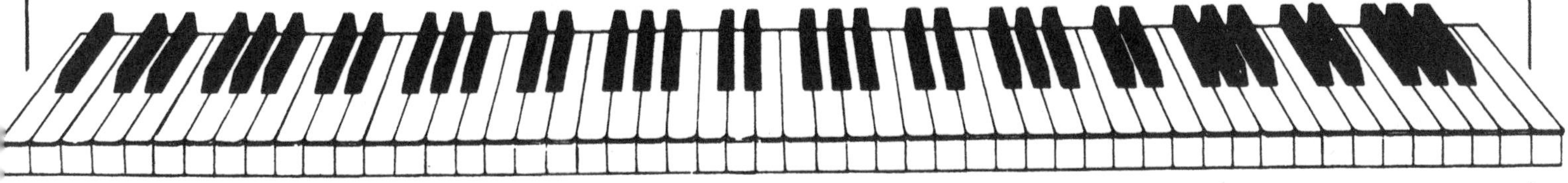

The keys on the keyboard are black and white.

Do you see the groups of 2 black keys and 3 black keys?
  With a red pencil circle the groups of 2 black keys.
  With another color circle the groups of 3 black keys.
  (You will find one black key left over. This is not important.)

Play all the groups of 2 black keys with any fingers, either hand.

Play all the groups of 3 black keys with any fingers, either hand.

Picture No. 2 --- NOTES

Notes are either black   ●   or white.   ○

Most notes have stems.

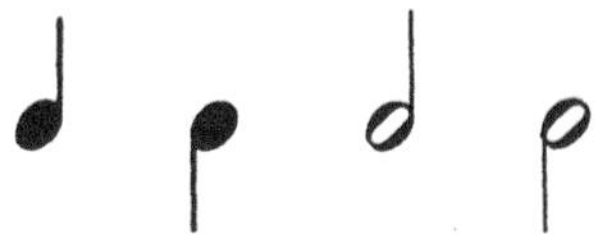

Stems may go either up or down from the note.

Notes tell us which keys to play on the piano and when to play them.

Picture No. 3 --- YOUR HANDS

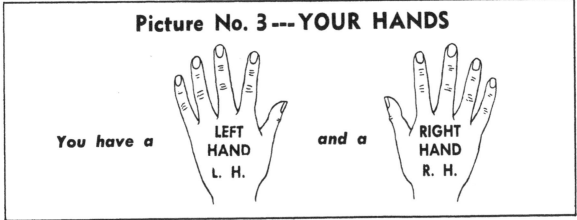

You have a   **LEFT HAND L. H.**   *and a*   **RIGHT HAND R. H.**

Now you are ready to learn to play your first piece.

W.M.Co. 11162

A STEADY PULSE
Higher

PRACTICE PLAN

1. Say the words and tap in a **musical rhythm** with your teacher.
2. Point to each note and sing the words as your teacher plays.
3. Sing and play the piece, yourself.

Play on the groups of 2 black keys, starting in the middle of the piano.
Use the middle finger of each hand. Brace the nail joint with your thumb.

Middle of
Keyboard

UP THE KEYBOARD

Play in march time

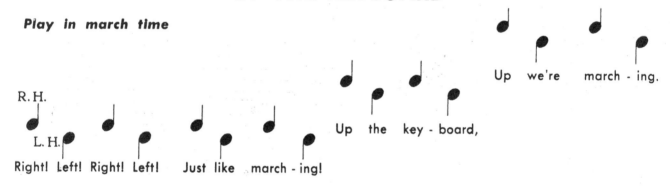

R.H.

L.H.

Right! Left! Right! Left!   Just like march-ing!   Up the key-board,   Up we're march-ing.

4. Did you keep a steady pulse?
5. Sing and play the piece 5 times each day for Home Work.

Circle the group of notes that sounded the **highest**.

> ### What have you learned?
> WHEN MUSIC **SOUNDS** HIGHER
> THE NOTES **LOOK** HIGHER ON THE PRINTED PAGE
> AND YOU **PLAY** HIGHER ON THE KEYBOARD.

Play the highest black key on the keyboard; the highest white key.
Play 3 black keys moving UP the keyboard; 3 white keys moving UP the keyboard.
Play a black key near the middle of the keyboard.

DUET FUN — TEACHER'S MUSIC

W.M.Co. 11162

A STEADY PULSE
Lower

PRACTICE PLAN

1. Say the words and tap in a **musical rhythm** with your teacher.
2. Point to each note and sing the words as your teacher plays.
3. Sing and play the piece, yourself.

Play on the groups of 2 black keys, starting in the middle of the piano.
Use the middle finger of each hand. Brace the nail joint with your thumb.

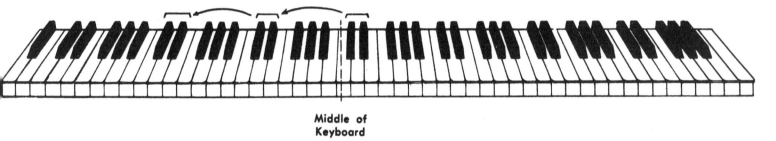

Middle of
Keyboard

DOWN THE KEYBOARD

Play in march time

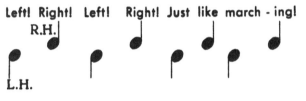

Left! Right! Left! Right! Just like march - ing!

Down the key - board,

Down we're march - ing.

4. Did you keep a steady pulse?
5. Sing and play the piece 5 times each day for Home Work.

Circle the group of notes that sounded the **lowest**.

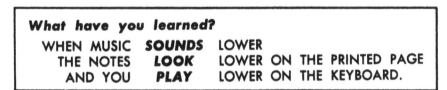

What have you learned?

WHEN MUSIC **SOUNDS** LOWER
THE NOTES **LOOK** LOWER ON THE PRINTED PAGE
AND YOU **PLAY** LOWER ON THE KEYBOARD.

Play the lowest black key on the keyboard; the lowest white key.
Play 3 black keys moving DOWN the keyboard; 3 white keys moving DOWN the keyboard.
Play a white key near the middle of the keyboard.

DUET FUN — TEACHER'S MUSIC

W.M.Co. 11162

QUARTER NOTES ♩ and HALF NOTES ♩

PRACTICE PLAN

1. Say the words and tap in a **musical rhythm*** with your teacher.
2. Point to each note and sing the words as your teacher plays.
3. Sing and play the piece, yourself.

Play on the groups of 2 black keys.
Use the middle finger of each hand. Brace the nail joint with your thumb.

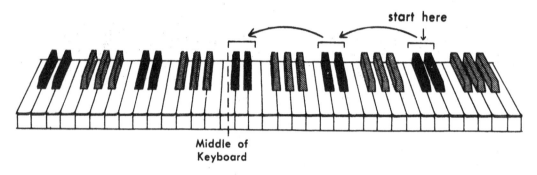

start here

Middle of
Keyboard

MY KITTY

Play softly and steadily

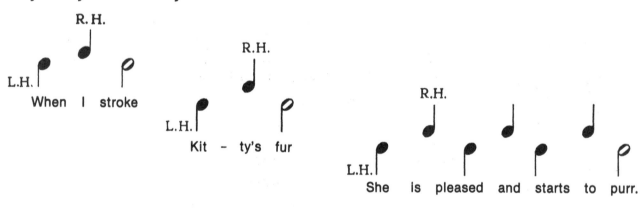

When   I   stroke

Kit – ty's   fur

She   is   pleased   and   starts   to   purr.

4. How many pulses did you feel on each ♩ _____? on each ♩ _____?
5. Did the second group of notes move UP or DOWN? The Third group?
6. Sing and play the piece 5 times each day for Home Work.

What have you learned?
A HALF NOTE gets 2 pulses
A QUARTER NOTE gets 1 pulse

$$\textit{o} = \textit{♩ ♩}$$

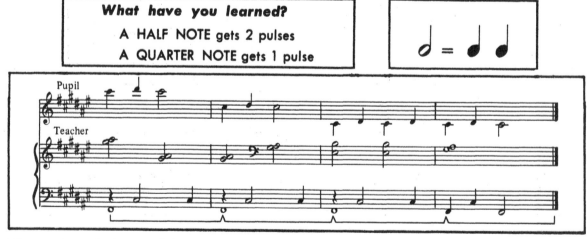

*Repeat the vowel sound of each syllable under half notes (or notes of longer duration) for as many pulses as the note re-ceives. Example:

When   I   stro-oke   Kit - ty's   fu - ur

UP-STEMS and DOWN-STEMS

PRACTICE PLAN

1. Say the words and tap in a **musical rhythm** with your teacher.
2. Point to each note and sing the words as your teacher plays.
3. Sing and play the piece, yourself.

Play on the groups of 2 black keys, starting in the middle of the piano.
Use the middle finger of each hand. Brace the nail joint with your thumb.

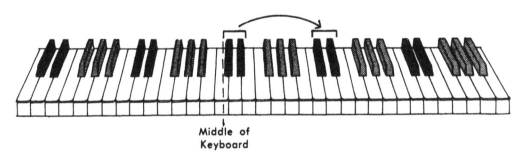

Middle of
Keyboard

TRAFFIC

Play loudly and steadily

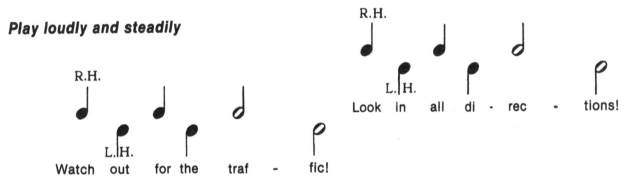

R.H.

L.H.
Look in all di - rec - tions!

R.H.

L.H.
Watch out for the traf - fic!

4. Which hand played the notes with up-stems?_____

   Which hand played the notes with down-stems?_____

5. Sing and play the piece 5 times each day for Home Work.

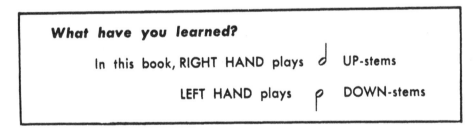

What have you learned?

In this book, RIGHT HAND plays UP-stems

LEFT HAND plays DOWN-stems

DUET FUN — TEACHER'S MUSIC

Pupil

Teacher

Close your eyes.

1. Can you HEAR when your teacher plays high on the keyboard? Low? In the middle?
2. Can you HEAR when your teacher plays loudly? Softly?
3. Feel and play the groups of 2 black keys all over the keyboard; the groups of 3 black keys.

W.M.Co. 11162

REVIEW: QUARTER NOTES and HALF NOTES
UP-STEMS and DOWN-STEMS

FOLLOW THE PRACTICE PLANS on pages 6 and 7.

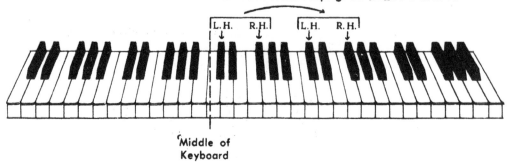

DRUM AND BUGLE CORPS

Play steadily

R.H.

L.H.

Drum   and   bug - le   corps

Drill - ing   just   out - side   the   door.

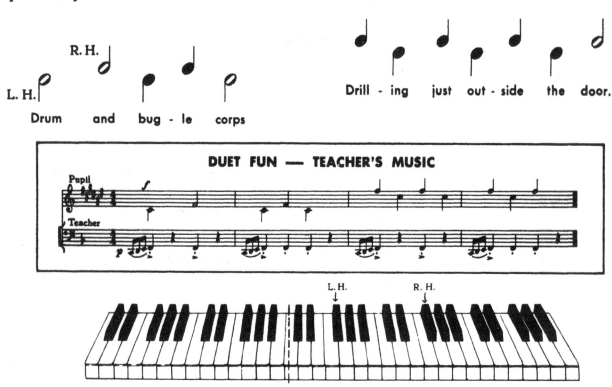

DUET FUN — TEACHER'S MUSIC

Pupil

Teacher

BLOW TRUMPET

Play loudly in march time

R.H.

Blow,   trum - pet!   Beat,   drum!   Let's   have   march - ing   mu - sic.

L.H.

DUET FUN — TEACHER'S MUSIC

Pupil

Teacher

W.M.Co. 11162

TEST YOURSELF

If you follow the rules you have learned in the PRACTICE PLANS, you will be able to play the following pieces without help.

Play on the groups of 2 black keys. Use the middle finger of each hand.

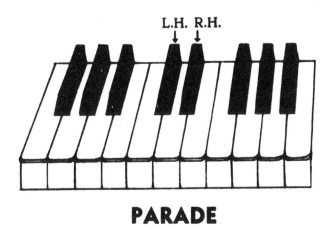

PARADE

Play in march time

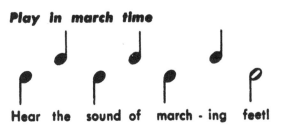

Hear the sound of march - ing feet!

They know how to keep the beat.

Did the second group of notes move UP or DOWN?
Which hand started each group of notes? _____

How many groups of notes do you see in the next piece?
Do they move UP or DOWN?
Which hand starts each group? _____

SNACK

Play with a steady pulse

When I'm hun-gry   Af - ter School,   Ap - ple pie   Sat - is - fies.

How many notes did the R. H. play? _____
How many notes did the L. H. play? _____

Unit 2

FINGER NUMBERS
Phrasing
Legato

Your Fingers Have Numbers

L.H.   R.H.

Touch your finger tips together
Move both 3rd fingers.
Move both 2nd fingers.
Move both 4th fingers.
Move both 5th fingers.
Move both 1st fingers.
Move R. H. 2nd finger.
Move L. H. 3rd finger.
Move L. H. 1st finger.
Move R. H. 4th finger.

A slur ⌒ groups notes together making a musical sentence which is called a PHRASE.

PRACTICE PLAN

1. Say and tap the words with your teacher.
2. Point to each note and sing the finger numbers as your teacher plays.
3. Before you play, touch the keys.
4. Play the notes under each slur firmly and smoothly, holding on to each key until you play the next. This is LEGATO playing.

Play on the groups of 3 black keys.

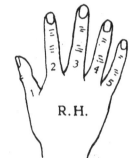

MUSIC LESSONS

Smoothly

This is fun!   This is fun!

Mu - sic les - sons have be - gun.

5. Sing and play the piece 5 times each day for Home Work.

DUET FUN — TEACHER'S MUSIC

Pupil

Teacher

PRACTICE PLAN

1. Say and tap the words with your teacher.
2. Point to each note and sing the finger numbers while your teacher plays.
3. Before you play, touch the keys.
4. Play the notes under each slur LEGATO.

Play on these keys.

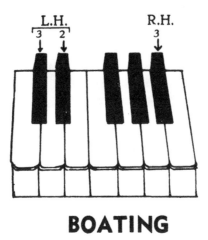

BOATING

Slowly and softly

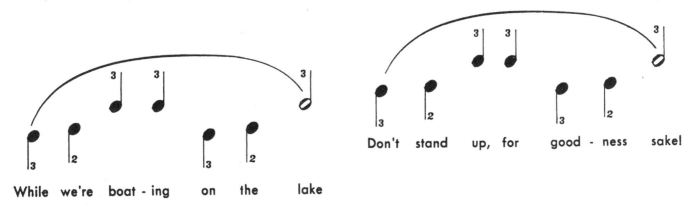

While we're boat - ing on the lake   Don't stand up, for good - ness sake!

5. Sing and play the piece 5 times each day for Home Work.

DUET FUN — TEACHER'S MUSIC

Close your eyes.

1. Can you **HEAR** when your teacher plays 3 keys moving UP? 3 keys moving DOWN?
2. Can you **SING** these tones when your teacher plays them near the middle of the keyboard?
3. When your teacher **plays** one of the 2 black keys, can you find the same tone BY EAR?
4. When your teacher **plays** one of the 3 black keys, can you find the same tone BY EAR?

W.M.Co. 11162

PRACTICE PLAN

1. Say and tap the words with your teacher.
2. Point to each note and sing the finger numbers while your teacher plays.
3. Before you play, touch the keys.
4. Play the notes under each slur LEGATO.

Play on these keys.

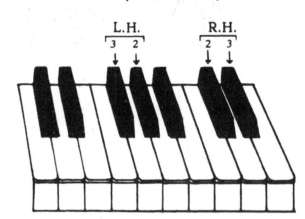

BROWN LEAVES

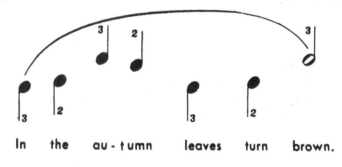

In the au-tumn leaves turn brown.

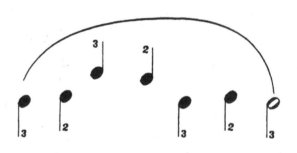

Win-ter winds will blow them down.

5. Sing and play the piece 5 times each day for Home Work.

What have you learned?

Firm, smooth playing is

_____PLAYING.

DUET FUN — TEACHER'S MUSIC

W.M.Co. 11162

THE MIDDLE OF THE KEYBOARD

The middle of the keyboard is a little to the left of the exact center.

In this book, a broken line will show you the middle of the keyboard.

Usually the L. H. plays all notes from the middle of the keyboard DOWNWARD.

Usually the R. H. plays all notes from the middle of the keyboard UPWARD.

PRACTICE PLAN

1. Say and tap the words with your teacher.

2. Point to each note and sing the finger numbers while your teacher plays.

3. Before you play, touch the keys. Then keep your eyes straight ahead on the notes. Do not look at your fingers. Play without stopping.

4. Play the notes over each slur LEGATO. A slur means the same, whether under or over notes.

5. Play the thumb on its side tip.

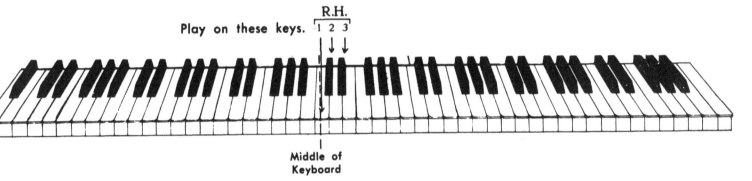

SINGING UP AND DOWN

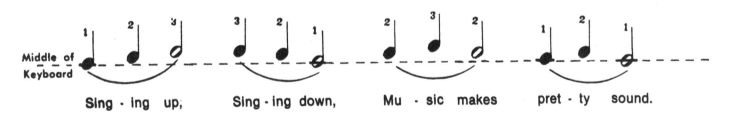

Sing - ing up;   Sing - ing down,   Mu - sic makes   pret - ty   sound.

6. Circle the notes with lines going through them. Which key did you play for these notes?

DUET FUN — TEACHER'S MUSIC

W.M.Co. 11162

A PIECE FOR LEFT HAND

PRACTICE PLAN

1. Say and tap the words with your teacher.
2. Point to each note and sing the finger numbers while your teacher plays.
3. Before you play, touch the keys.
4. Play the notes under each slur LEGATO.
5. Play the thumb on its side tip.

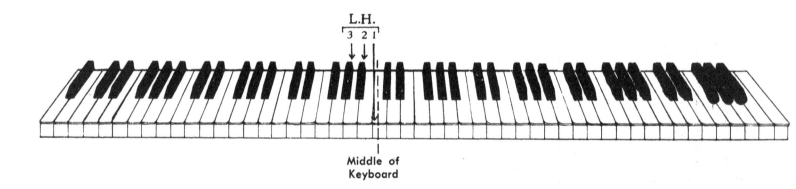

Middle of Keyboard

MERRILY WE ROLL ALONG

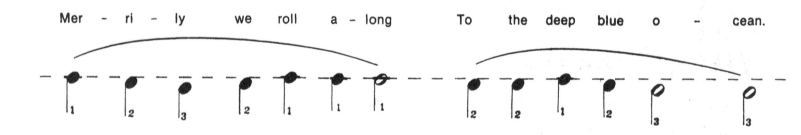

Mer – ri – ly   we   roll   a – long   To   the   deep   blue   o –   cean.

6. Circle the notes with lines going through them. Which key did you play for these notes?

DUET FUN — TEACHER'S MUSIC

Pupil

Teacher

PRACTICE PLAN

1. Say and tap the words with your teacher.

2. Point to each note and sing the finger numbers while your teacher plays.

3. Before you play, touch the keys. Then keep your eyes straight ahead on the notes. Do not look at your fingers. Play without stopping.

4. Play the notes under each slur LEGATO.

Play on these keys.

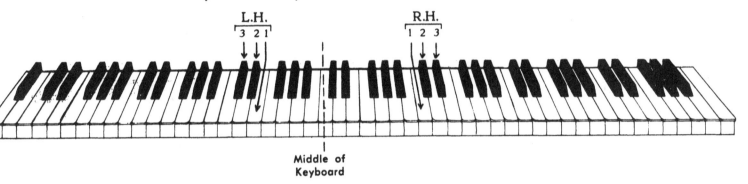

LULLABY

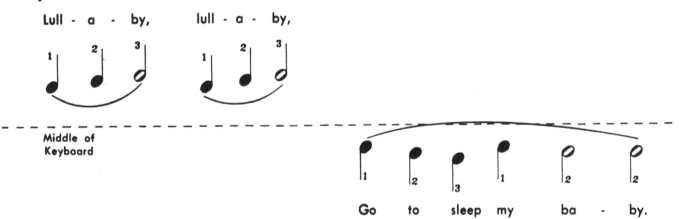

5. Sing and play the piece 5 times each day for Home Work.

TEST YOURSELF

If you follow the rules you have learned in the Practice Plans, you will be able to play the following pieces without any help.

Play on these keys.

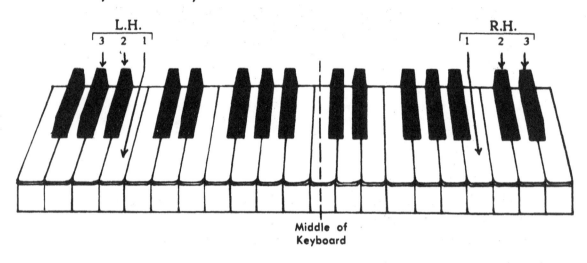

Middle of Keyboard

HALLOWE'EN

In a spooky manner

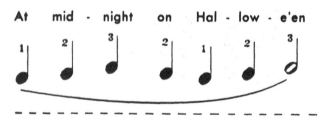

At mid - night on Hal - low - e'en

(Middle of Keyboard)

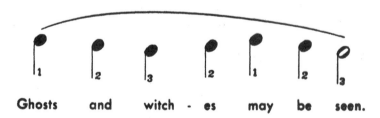

Ghosts and witch - es may be seen.

DUET FUN — TEACHER'S MUSIC

Pupil

Teacher

W.M.Co. 11162

Unit 3
THE WHITE KEYS

Check the 3 white keys which are neighbors of the groups of 2 black keys.
Play these white keys with any finger, either hand, all over the keyboard.

Example

PRACTICE PLAN

1. Say and tap the words.

2. Look at the notes. Do the lines help you to see when the notes move UP or DOWN, or when the same note REPEATS?

3. Circle any REPEATED notes you see. How can you tell if a note is repeated?

4. Circle the first R. H. note. Do you see the same note written again?

5. Circle the lowest note in the piece.

6. A slur printed under a group of notes means the same as when it is above a group of notes.

Play on these keys.

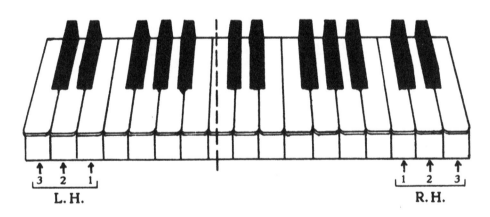

L. H.   R. H.

BIRTHDAY

Happily

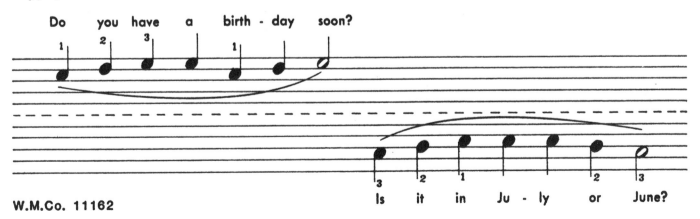

Do you have a birth - day soon?

Is it in Ju - ly or June?

W.M.Co. 11162

Check the 4 white keys which are neighbors of the groups of 3 black keys.

Play these white keys with any finger, either hand, all over the keyboard.

Example

PRACTICE PLAN

1. Say and tap the words.
2. Circle the highest note in each group.
3. How many notes have lines going through them? ____
4. How many notes are in spaces between 2 lines? ____
5. Do you see any notes on the same space? On the same line?

Play on these keys.

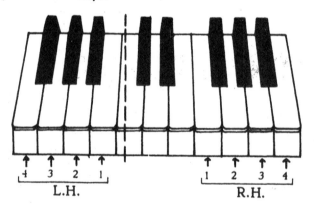

4 3 2 1   1 2 3 4
L.H.   R.H.

A RAINY DAY

Very softly and slowly

gent - ly fall - ing;   Soft - ly call - ing.

Mist - y rain is   Lone - ly birds are

DUET FUN — TEACHER'S MUSIC

soft pedal. also

W.M.Co. 11162

PRACTICE PLAN

1. Say and tap the words.
2. Circle the highest note in each group.
3. How many notes have lines going through them? _____
4. How many notes are in spaces between 2 lines? _____
5. Do you see any notes on the same space? On the same line?

Play on these keys.

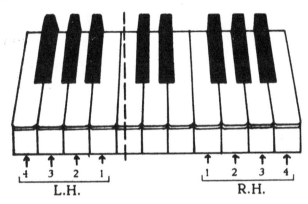

SNOW FLAKES

Gently

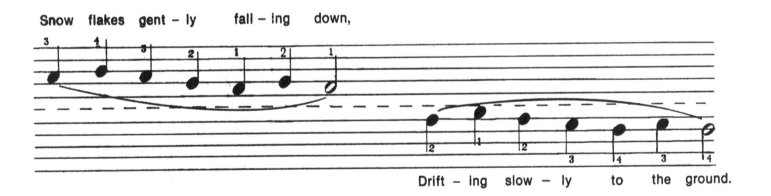

Snow flakes gent - ly fall - ing down,

Drift - ing slow - ly to the ground.

DUET FUN — TEACHER'S MUSIC

*Pupil's notes will be played 1 octave higher.

THE MUSICAL ALPHABET

The white keys on the keyboard have the same names as the first seven letters of the alphabet, and they repeat over and over.

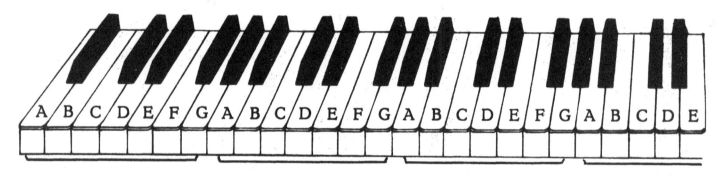

With any fingers, either hand, play A-B-C-D-C-F-G all over the keyboard.

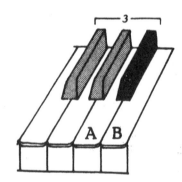

A and B are neighbors of the highest key of the group of 3 black keys.

Play A and B as many places on the keyboard as you can, forward and backward, saying their names.

C, D and E are neighbors of the groups of 2 black keys.

Play C-D-E as many places on the keyboard as you can, forward and backward, saying their names.

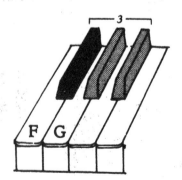

F and G are neighbors of the lowest key of the group of 3 black keys.

Play F and G as many places on the keyboard as you can, forward and backward, saying their names.

W.M.Co. 11162

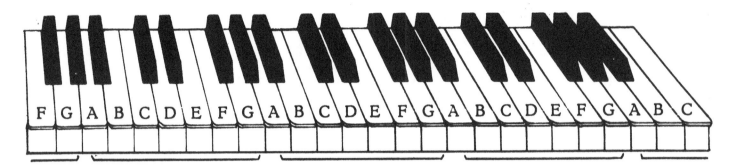

F G A B C D E F G A B C D E F G A B C D E F G A B C

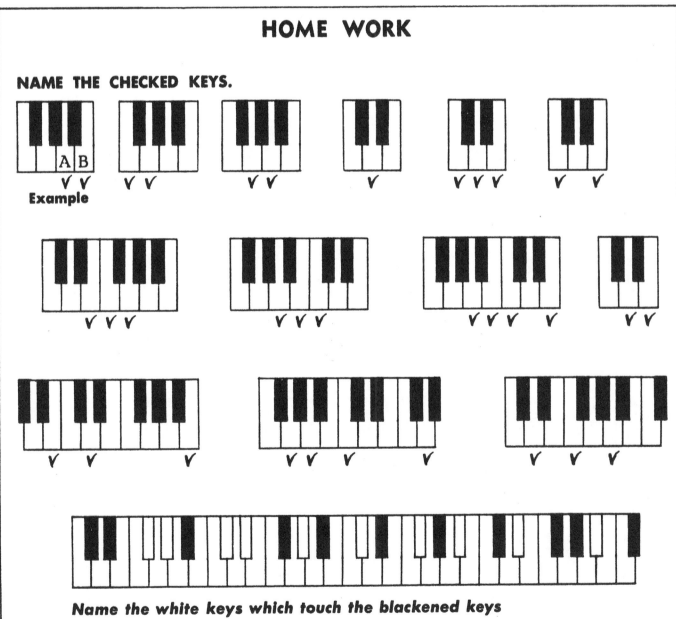

HOME WORK

NAME THE CHECKED KEYS.

A B
✔ ✔
Example

Name the white keys which touch the blackened keys above.

It is important to memorize the musical alphabet both _FORWARD_ and _BACKWARD_.

When you say the letters forward, you are moving UP the keyboard.

When you say the letters backward, you are moving DOWN the keyboard.

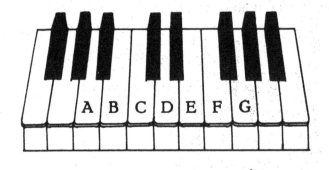

Play and say up the keyboard.

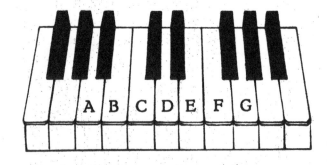

Play and say down the keyboard.

HOME WORK

———————→ = Write the key names up the keyboard.

←——————— = Write the key names down the keyboard.

PRACTICE PLAN

1. Say and tap the words.
2. Do you see any REPEATED notes?
3. How many notes have lines going through them? _____
4. How many notes are in spaces between lines? _____

Write the letter names of the keys you will play.

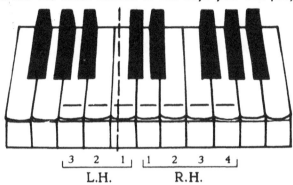

What is the name of the key in the middle of the keyboard? ____

This key is often called MIDDLE ____. In the piece below, this key is played 3 times. Can you find the NOTES which tell you to play this key?

OUR ALPHABET

Moderately slowly, with a firm touch

D, E, F, G, is the mu - sic al - pha - bet.

A, B, C,

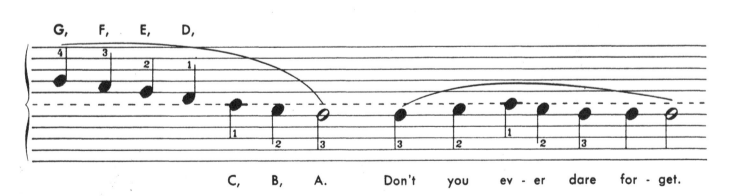

G, F, E, D,

C, B, A. Don't you ev - er dare for - get.

> A **brace** helps to guide your eyes to the next line of music.

W.M.Co. 11162

TEST YOURSELF

Write the letter names of the keys you will play

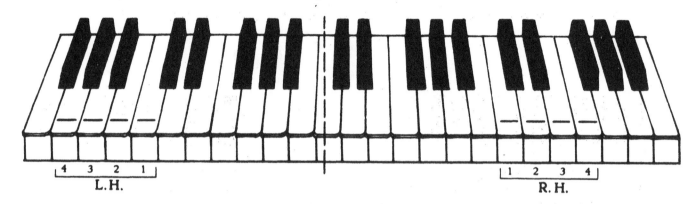

If you follow the rules of the Practice Plans, you will be able to play the following piece without any help.

MIRROR, MIRROR

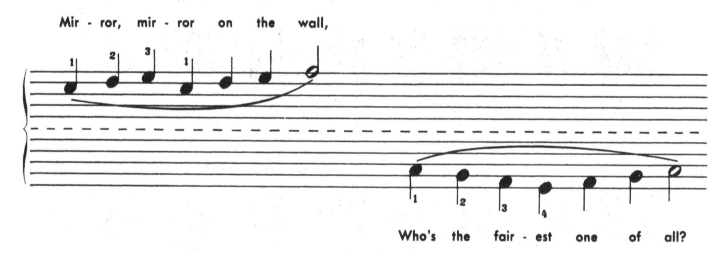

Mir - ror, mir - ror on the wall,

Who's the fair - est one of all?

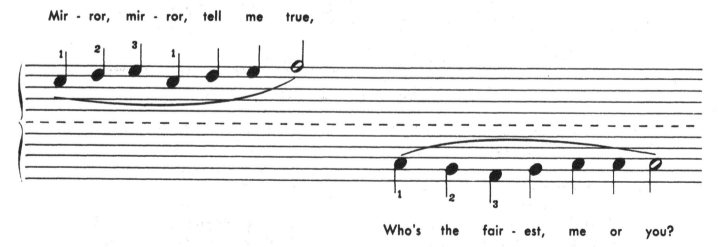

Mir - ror, mir - ror, tell me true,

Who's the fair - est, me or you?

Close your eyes.

1. When your teacher plays C-D-E different places on the keyboard can you find the same tones?

2. Can you do the same with A-B-C? E-F-G?

3. Can you sing these tones as your teacher plays?

W.M.Co. 11162

Unit 4

STEPS, SKIPS AND REPEATS ON THE WHITE KEYS.

1. When you move up or down the keyboard on neighbor keys, you are moving by STEPS.

2. When you move up or down the keyboard skipping keys, you are moving by SKIPS.

3. When you play the same key, you are REPEATING.

NEIGHBOR LETTERS are always STEPS
on the keyboard.

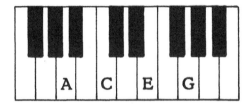

SKIPPED LETTERS are always SKIPS
on the keyboard.

On the keyboard below, write the names of the white keys moving downward by STEPS.

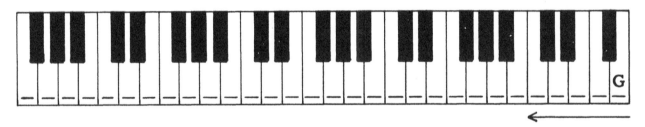

On the keyboard below, write the names of the white keys moving upward by SKIPS.

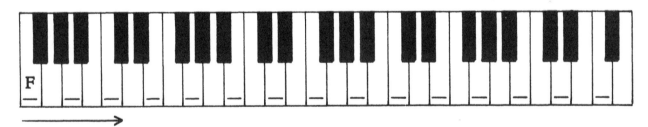

WRITE THE ANSWER

1. A step up from C is _____.
2. A step down from E is _____.
3. A skip down from E is _____.
4. A step down from F is _____.
5. A step down from G is _____.
6. A skip up from D is _____.
7. A step down from B is _____.
8. A skip down from C is _____.
9. A skip up from A is _____.
10. A skip up from E is _____.

1. A step down from _____ is D.
2. A skip down from _____ is C.
3. A skip up from _____ is A.
4. A step up from _____ is A.
5. A step down from _____ is B.
6. A skip down from _____ is G.
7. A skip down from _____ is F.
8. A step up from _____ is G.
9. A skip up from _____ is C.
10. A skip up from _____ is F.

W.M.Co. 11162

SAY THE ANSWER

Touch these keys:

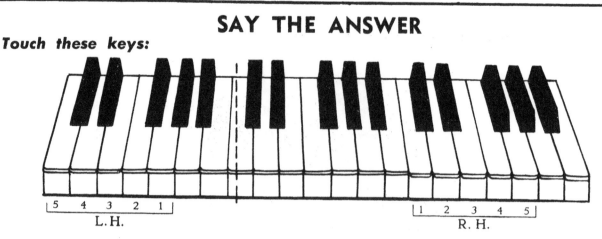

5 4 3 2 1
L. H.

1 2 3 4 5
R. H.

First, with the L.H., then, with the R.H., play and say the answer: "a step up" "a step down", "a skip up", "a skip down". (DO NOT LOOK AT YOUR FINGERS.)

Example:

1. Play C. **You say:**	1. Play C.	1. Play G.
2. Play D ("a step up")	2. Play E (?)	2. Play E (?)
3. Play F ("a skip up")	3. Play G (?)	3. Play F (?)
4. Play E ("a step down")	4. Play F (?)	4. Play D (?)

Touch the same keys. First, with the L.H.; then, with the R.H., play the finger which is indicated and say the name of the key you are playing.

Example for the R.H.:

1. Play 1st finger (C)	1. Play 5 (?)	1. Play 3 (?)
2. Play 3rd finger (E)	2. Play 1 (?)	2. Play 2 (?)
3. Play 4th finger (F)	3. Play 2 (?)	3. Play 4 (?)
4. Play 5th finger (G)	4. Play 4 (?)	4. Play 3 (?)

PRACTICE PLAN

1. Say and tap the words.
2. Look at the notes. Do the lines and spaces help you see when the notes move up or down, or when the same note repeats?
3. How can you tell if a note is repeated? Circle any repeated notes you see.
4. How can you tell the difference between repeated notes and notes that are stepping up or down?
5. Before you play, touch the keys. Then keep your eyes straight ahead on the notes. Do not look at your fingers. Play straight through without stopping.

Write the letter names of the keys you will play.

1 2 3 4 5
R. H.

STEP BY STEP
(FOR R.H.)
In moderate time

Up the key - board step by step. Then back down with lots of pep.

Play the piece again, singing the letter names of the keys instead of the words.

W.M.Co. 11162

Following the same practice plan, play STEP BY STEP with your L.H.

Write the letter names of the keys you will play.

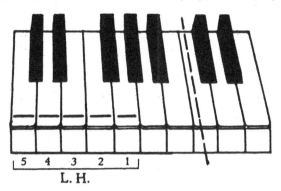

STEP BY STEP
(FOR L. H.)

In moderate time

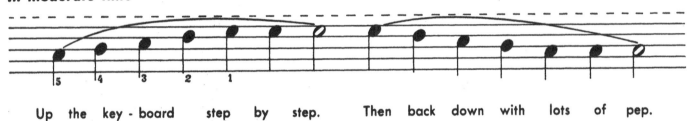

Up the key-board step by step. Then back down with lots of pep.

STEP BY STEP
(FOR BOTH HANDS)

In moderate time

Up the key-board step by step. Then back down with lots of pep.

Play STEP BY STEP again, singing the letter names of the keys instead of the words.

On the keyboard below, write the names of the white keys moving downward by SKIPS.

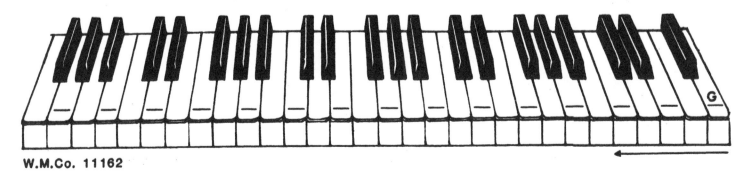

W.M.Co. 11162

PRACTICE PLAN

1. Say and tap the words.
2. Look at the notes. Circle any repeated notes you see.
3. How do the notes in this piece **look** different from the notes in STEP BY STEP? **Do any of these notes have lines going through them?**
4. How can you tell the difference between notes that move by Steps and notes that move by Skips?
5. Before you play, touch the keys. Then keep your eyes straight ahead on the notes. Do not look at your fingers. Play straight through without stopping.

Write the letter names of the keys you will play.

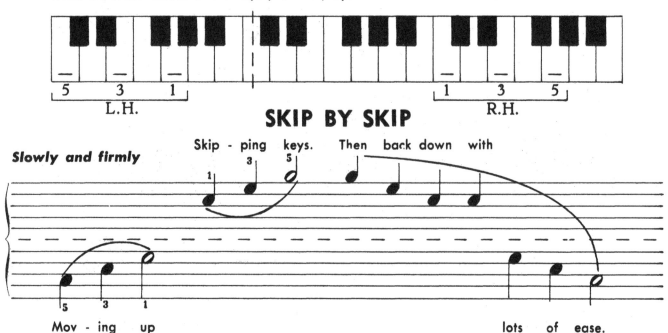

SKIP BY SKIP

Following the Practice Plan above, play SKIP BY SKIP on different keys.

Write the letter names of the keys you will play.

SKIP BY SKIP

> **What have you learned?**
> SKIPPING NOTES skip either from a **space** to a **space** or from a **line** to a **line**

TEST YOURSELF

If you follow the rules of the Practice Plans, you will be able to play the following pieces without any help.

Write the letter names of the keys you will play.

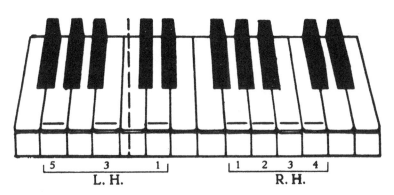

SKIPS AND STEPS

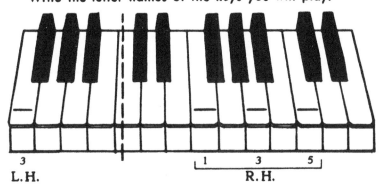

Some re - peat. Step - ping makes this song com - plete.

Some notes skip and

Write the letter names of the keys you will play.

PARADE

Don't you love a big bass drum?

Rum, tum, Rum, tum, tum.

Close your eyes.

1. Can you HEAR when your teacher plays steps or skips or repeated notes?

2. Can you sing a step up from Middle C? A skip up from Middle C?

Unit 5
LINE NOTES AND SPACE NOTES

Notes are printed on lines and spaces.

A note with a line going through it is called a LINE NOTE.

Example:

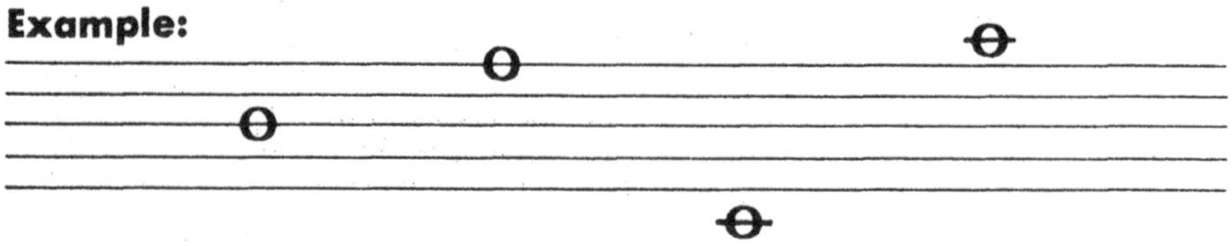

A note which does not have a line going through it is called a SPACE NOTE.

Example:

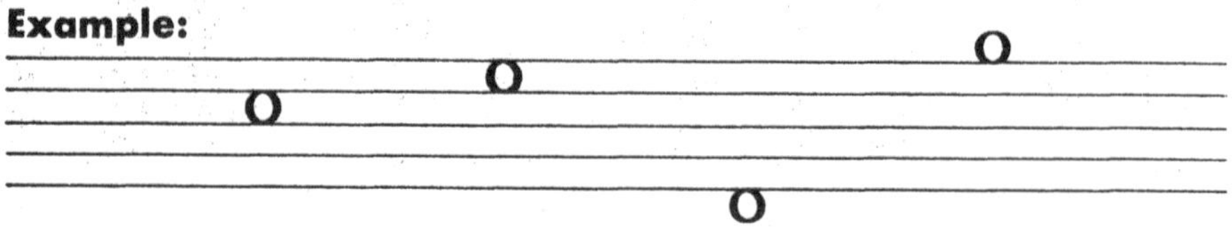

It is important to be able to recognize LINE NOTES and SPACE NOTES quickly.

HOME WORK

Write L for all line notes.
Write S for all space notes.

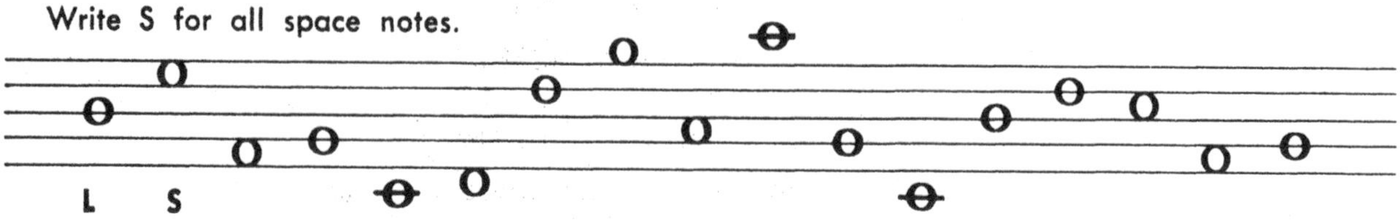

L   S

Draw line and space notes below:

S   L   S   S   L   S   L   L   S   L   L   S   L   S

Draw half notes below:

L   L   S   L   S   S   S   L   S   L   L   L   S   L

Draw quarter notes below:

S   S   L   S   S   S   L   L   S   L   S   S   L   L

LINE NOTES and SPACE NOTES moving up the keyboard by steps.

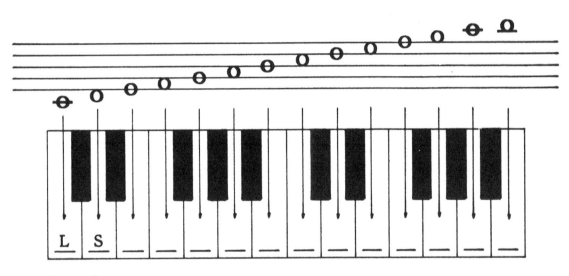

Example:

Write L on the keys for LINE NOTES.

Write S on the keys for SPACE NOTES.

Color all the line notes and line keys red.

Color all the space notes and space keys blue.

Does this make a pattern you can describe?

Draw line and space notes moving up the keyboard by steps. Draw a note for each white key directly above the arrows.

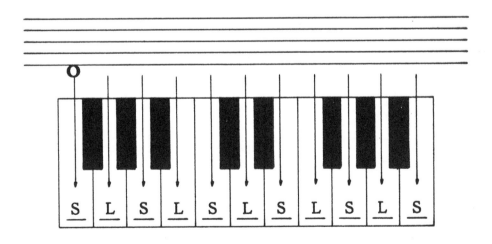

Reading Notes by STEPS, SKIPS and REPEATS

Here are 5 notes moving up on lines and spaces by STEPS.

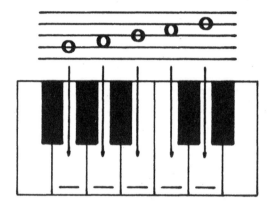

1. Color the line notes and line keys red.
2. Color the space notes and space keys blue.

3. Write the names of the keys.

---

1. Copy the 5 notes above with a pencil.

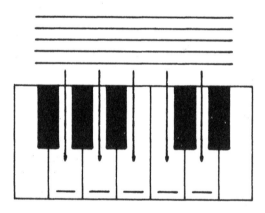

2. Erase the 2nd and 4th notes.

3. Copy the letter names of the keys.

4. Erase the letter names of the notes you erased.

Now, play the three notes which remain.

1. Did you play STEPS or SKIPS?
2. Did you erase line notes or space notes?

---

1. Copy the same five notes with a pencil.

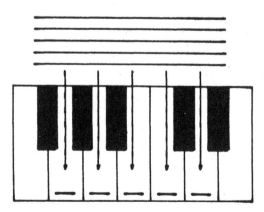

2. Erase only the 3rd note.
3. Write the letter names of the keys.
4. Erase the letter name of the note you erased.

Now, play the 4 notes which remain.

1. Which notes step? Which notes skip?
2. Did you erase a line note or a space note?

W.M.Co. 11162

Here are 5 different notes moving up on lines and spaces by STEPS.

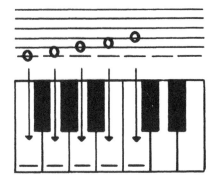

1. Color the line notes and line keys red.
2. Color the space notes and space keys blue.

3. Write the names of the keys.
4. Can you find the first note on the keyboard?
5. Play the notes.

---

1. Copy the 5 notes above with a pencil.

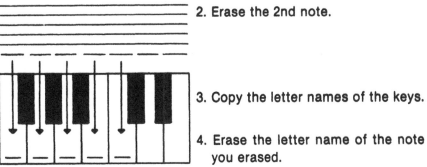

2. Erase the 2nd note.

3. Copy the letter names of the keys.

4. Erase the letter name of the note you erased.

Now, play the four notes which remain.
1. Which notes skip? Which notes step?
2. Did you erase a line note or a space note?

Here is a different keyboard picture.

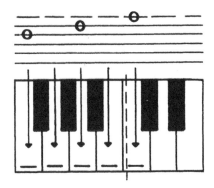

1. Are the 3 printed notes line notes or space notes?
2. Draw the 2 missing notes above the arrows. Are these notes space notes or line notes?

3. Write the names of the keys.
4. Can you find the fifth note on the keyboard?
5. Play the 5 notes.

W.M.Co. 11162

When a note is printed again on the same line or space it is called a REPEATED NOTE, and you play the same key again.

Example:

Repeated notes on a line   Repeated notes on a space

Draw 2 repeated notes after each of the printed notes below.

HOME WORK

1. In the exercise below, color the line notes red and the space notes blue.

2. Write a — (minus sign) for a STEP, a + (plus sign) for a SKIP and an R for a REPEAT.

    —   +   R   —   —   —   —

Example:

    —   —   —   —

1. From each of the given notes below, draw a note:

A step up   A skip up   A step down   A step up   A skip down   A skip up   A step up

Example:

A skip down   A step down   A step up   A skip up   A skip up   A step down   a step up

DOTTED HALF NOTES 𝅗𝅥.

PRACTICE PLAN

1. Say and tap the words.
2. How many pulses did you feel on each dotted half note?
3. Look at the notes for STEPS, SKIPS and REPEATS.
4. Before you play, touch the keys. Then keep your eyes straight ahead on the notes. Do not look at your fingers. Play straight through without stopping.

Write the letter names of the keys you will play.

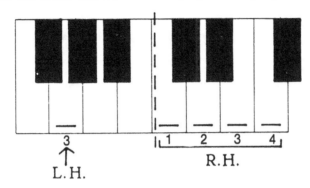

L.H. R.H.

A WALTZ

With a gay lilt

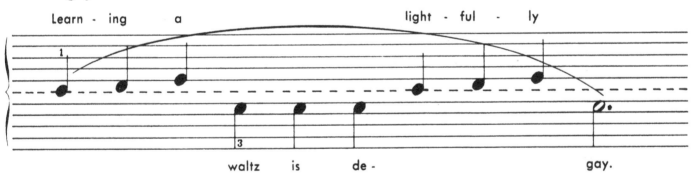

Learn - ing a light - ful - ly
waltz is de - gay.

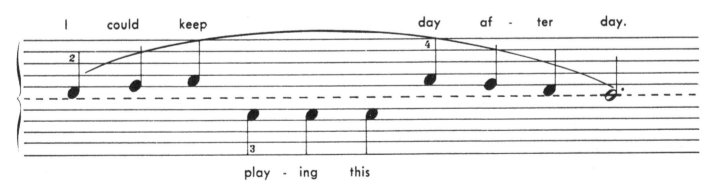

I could keep day af - ter day.
play - ing this

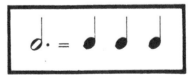

What have you learned?
A dotted half note gets 3 pulses.

*DUET FUN: Pupil plays the piece on the next keys of the same name UP the keyboard. The musical term for this is ONE OCTAVE HIGHER.

*DUET FUN — TEACHER'S MUSIC

Teacher
mp lightly

PRACTICE PLAN

1. Say and tap the rhythm.

2. How many dotted half notes do you see?

3. Look at the notes for STEPS, SKIPS and REPEATS.

4. Before you play, touch the keys. Then keep your eyes straight ahead on the notes. Do not look at your fingers. Play straight through without stopping.

Write the letter names of the keys you will play.

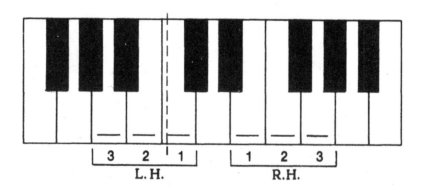

BALLET CLASS

Gracefully

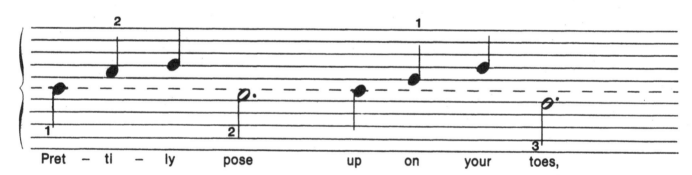

Pret – ti – ly   pose   up   on   your   toes,

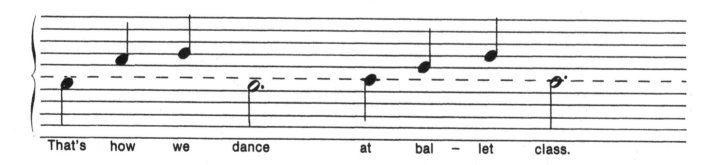

That's   how   we   dance   at   bal – let   class.

DUET FUN — TEACHER'S MUSIC

W.M.Co. 11162

WHOLE NOTES

PRACTICE PLAN

1. Say and tap the words.
2. How many pulses did you feel on each whole note?
3. Look at the notes for STEPS, SKIPS, and REPEATS.
4. Before you play, touch the keys. Then keep your eyes straight ahead on the notes. Do not look at your fingers. Play straight through without stopping.

Write the letter names of the keys you will play.

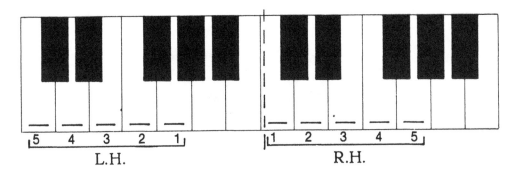

L.H.   R.H.

Happlly

PLAYGROUND

On the play - ground   at our school

there   are   slides   and   swings.

At re - cess   we   all   go   out   and

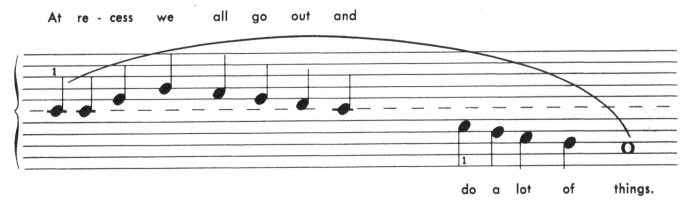

do   a   lot   of   things.

What have you learned?
A whole not gets 4 pulses.

DUET FUN — TEACHER'S MUSIC

Teacher

W.M.Co. 11162

PRACTICE PLAN

1. Say and tap the words.

2. How many whole notes do you see?

3. Look at the notes for STEPS, SKIPS and REPEATS.

4. Before you play, touch the keys. Then keep your eyes straight ahead on the notes. Do not look at your fingers. Play straight through without stopping.

Write the letter names of the keys you will play.

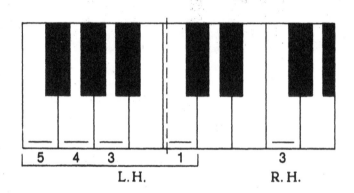

5　4　3　1　L.H.　　3　R.H.

THE KING'S FANFARE

Slowly, loudly　　　　　　　　　　　　　　　　sound!

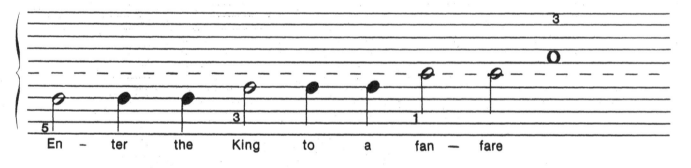

En — ter the King to a fan — fare

Take off your

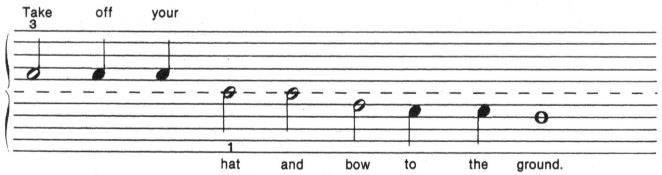

hat and bow to the ground.

DUET FUN — TEACHER'S MUSIC

TEST YOURSELF

If you follow the rules of the Practice Plans, you will be able to play the following piece without any help.

Write the letter names of the keys you will play.

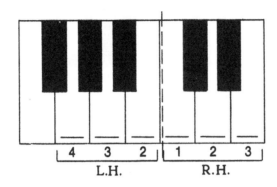

AT CHURCH

Joyfully

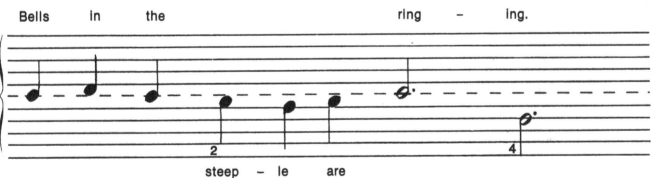

Bells   in   the   ring — ing.

steep - le   are

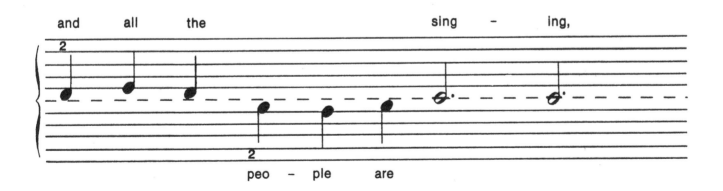

and   all   the   sing — ing,

peo - ple   are

TEST YOURSELF

If you follow the rules of the Practice Plans, you will be able to play the following piece without any help.

Write the letter names of the keys you will play.

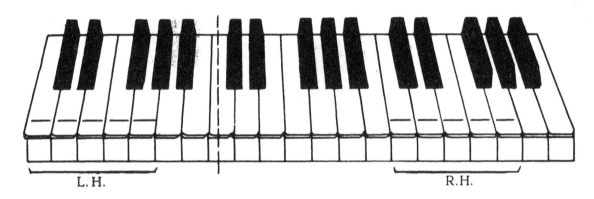

SLEEPY HEAD

Sleepily

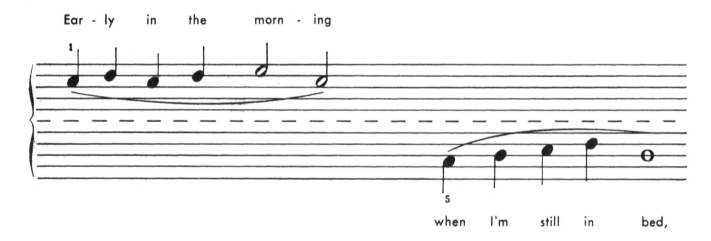

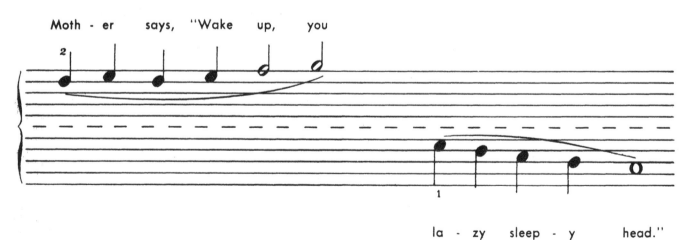

W.M.Co. 11162